OOPS! I Did It (Again)!

by Robin Wasserman

Illustrated by Angela Martini

SCHOLASTIC INC.

New York   Toronto   London   Auckland   Sydney
Mexico City   New Delhi   Hong Kong   Buenos Aires

*For Brandon McGlynn and
David and Natalie Roher,
the best cousins ever!*

ISBN 0-439-55608-2

Copyright © 2003 by Scholastic Inc.
All rights reserved. Published by Scholastic Inc.
SCHOLASTIC and associated logos are trademarks
and/or registered trademarks of Scholastic Inc.

10 9 8 7 6 5 4 3 2   3 4 5 6 7 8/0

Printed in the U.S.A.
First printing, October 2003

BOOK DESIGN BY JENNIFER RINALDI WINDAU

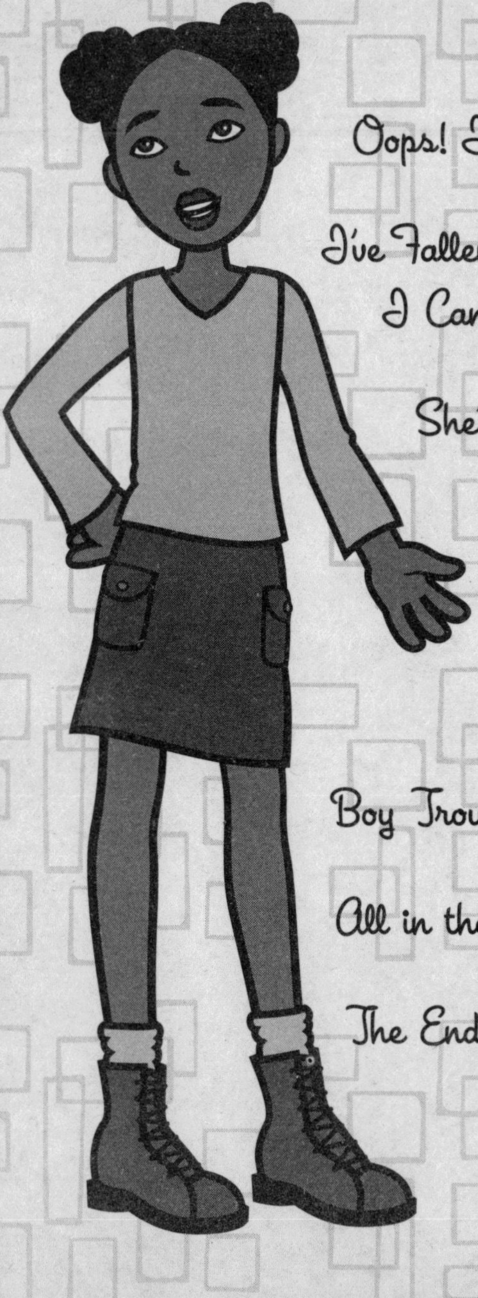

OOPS!
I Did It
(Again)!

You've done it again—you've embarrassed yourself in front of everyone and you don't know what to do. You're probably asking, Why me? Why is the world out to get me? Why did I slip in the mud or drop my tray in the cafeteria or sneeze all over that cute boy? (At least, he *was* cute before he was covered in mucus.) Why is everyone laughing at me—and when are they going to stop?

Soon. You can count on it.

Take a deep breath. Fortunately, being embarrassed doesn't come with a life sentence. Most people are too worried about their own lives (and their own embarrassments) to spend too much time worrying about yours. Which means they'll soon forget the humiliating day you burned off

5

your hair in science class and—as soon as the hair grows back—you'll probably forget about it, too. Or at least you'll be able to laugh about it with your friends (as soon as you start speaking to them again).

But what do you do in the meantime? What do you do when it seems like the whole world is laughing at you? Here's an idea: Hold your head high and pretend you don't care (even if you care more than anything in the world). Try to stop thinking about it—and remember that every single person in that laughing crowd has had hideous moments, possibly even worse than yours.

Don't believe it? This book is full of humiliating moments that other kids have had to suffer through. And maybe by the time you're done laughing at them, everyone else will be done laughing at you!

I've Fallen and I Can't Get Up

Face it: Some people are clumsy. They drop things. They break things. They fall down, and they usually bring others down with them. Maybe this person is you.

Or maybe you're graceful and have had only one moment of klutziness in your entire life—but unfortunately, that moment took place in front of every single person you've ever met.

Whatever happened, it couldn't be as bad as what happened to these kids . . . right?

Humiliation Factor

 KINDA KLUTZY

 OOPS . . . OUCH!

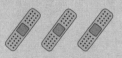 WATCH OUT WORLD, HERE I COME!

 DISASTER WAITING TO HAPPEN

A PERFECT 10

When my friends invited me to go ice-skating, I went along, even though I'm not very good. A really cute boy I liked was coming, and I wanted to impress him. I was skating well, so I decided to show off a little—I tried to skate backward. Bad idea. I skated backward about ten inches—then I fell down and slid for another ten feet! The worst part was that I knocked down a bunch of people on my way—it was a giant people pileup, and the boy I was trying to impress was right on the bottom!

I've never seen that move in the Olympics!

Nikki

ON A ROLL

I was at my school's awards ceremony, ready to collect my sports award. My name was called, and I got up to walk down the aisle. About halfway to the stage, I tripped, fell, and actually *rolled* down the aisle! If you didn't think this was possible, trust me, it is. As if that wasn't bad enough, I had to pick myself up and get up onstage in front of everyone to accept the award!

Cynthia

HUMILIATION HELPER:

Okay, you've fallen and you can get up—but you don't want to. You know you'll just have to face the crowd of people laughing their heads off at your spectacular slipup. What now?

Well, there's the head-down, face-bright-red, slink-away-as-fast-as-possible approach. It's an easy out, but is guaranteed to leave echoes of laughter ringing in your ears for the rest of the day.

Why not try a bolder move? Stand up, dust yourself off, look those laughers right in the face, and grin. Take a bow and raise your arms in triumph. People may still spend the rest of the day talking about your hilarious fall—but they'll also be talking about the hilariously cool way you handled it!

THE WEAKEST LINK

I was playing tug-of-war at summer camp. I was at the head of my team, facing off with a cute guy from the boys' bunk. There was a giant pit of mud between us. My side was about to win when my foot slid and I lost my balance. Without my help, the rest of my team couldn't hold the rope. The other team pulled us all into the mud pit! We were totally covered in mud, and it was all my fault. But I got my revenge. When the captain of the other team reached over to help me out, I pulled him in, too!

Liz

PARTY ON

I had bought a new dress and new shoes—and I was going to wear them to this party, no matter what. The weather was snowy and icy, and my mother thought I should wear boots instead. But no way! I walked to the party in my new shoes—I may have been freezing, but I looked awesome. There was just one problem: My new shoes weren't really meant for walking through snow and ice. I was almost at the party when I slipped and fell into a giant snowbank. I showed up at the party in my new shoes and new dress—completely dirty and soaking wet. I hate it when my mother is right!

Moms are always *right!*

Leslie

STRIKE!

My teacher hates it when we're late for class, so I was running down the hall, trying to make it to my desk before the bell rang. Since I was wearing muddy sneakers, maybe this wasn't such a good idea. As I ran down the last hallway, I slipped and fell onto my stomach. Then I slid the rest of the way and barreled into our school librarian. The books she had been carrying fell everywhere, including on top of me! The hallway has windows on both sides, so everyone saw me—they said it was like watching a human bowling ball!

Corey

DO YOU WANT FRIES WITH THAT?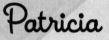

Our teachers usually don't eat lunch in the student cafeteria, and now I know why. We only get twenty minutes for lunch, so I was hurrying back to my table with my tray of food. I was going so fast that I didn't even notice my English teacher walking by in the other direction. But she sure noticed me—especially when I accidentally slammed into her and knocked her to the floor! I lost my balance, too, and dropped my tray on top of her. Poor Mrs. Donovan had mustard, ketchup, and lettuce all over her face and hair!

Patricia

DANCER DISASTER

I take dance lessons at the same studio where our city ballet company rehearses. I'm always hoping that I'll run into a celebrity. One day, I got my wish. A famous dancer was performing with the company that weekend, and she stopped by to watch our dance class. I couldn't believe it was actually her! We all tried to impress her, especially me. When I leaped across the floor for my solo, I leaped extra high—and when I tripped, I fell extra hard. They had to call an ambulance— I had broken my ankle! At least I know that the famous dancer isn't going to forget me any time soon.

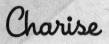

Charise

BOTTOMS UP

The stairs at my school are always filled with trash. It's totally disgusting. And also—as I found out the hard way—not too safe. I was running down the steps to get to class when I suddenly slipped on a banana peel! I thought that only happened in the movies, but it actually happened to me! My feet went flying up and I bounced down the rest of the steps to the bottom on *my* bottom. It hurt a lot, but not as much as it hurt my pride—especially because I was wearing a skirt that day. By the time I made it to the bottom, the skirt was up around my waist—and everyone was there to see!

Ashley

How would YOU rate this humiliation horror story? _____

15

She's Got the Look

Everyone's looking at you. And laughing. And you have no idea why. You think about it for a second—no, you haven't done anything funny. And you haven't *said* anything funny. You check again—yep, they're definitely laughing at you. So what's the deal?

Then you get it. There's something on your head or on your face or on your clothes—or maybe you're missing some clothes! Whatever's wrong with the way you look, you'd better figure it out and fix it—right away. Beauty may only be skin deep, but embarrassment goes all the way down!

Humiliation Factor

Q YOU LOOKIN' AT ME?

Q Q HOW COULD YOU HAVE LET ME GO OUT LOOKING LIKE *THIS*?

Q Q Q I'LL NEVER SHOW MY FACE AROUND HERE AGAIN

Q Q Q Q TIME TO CHANGE MY NAME AND MOVE OUT OF TOWN

16

FREE AT LAST

In second grade, I played the Statue of Liberty in our "March of Freedom" pageant. My mother had made my costume out of a green sheet—it was pinned at my shoulder. At least, it was pinned there until the middle of the show, when the pin popped open and the sheet fell off. I was left onstage with just my torch and my underwear!

Susie

Give her your tired, your poor—oh, forget about that, give the girl some real clothes!

A STICKY SITUATION

I was in the art room during lunch, working on my final project. I was making a collage and using an incredibly sticky glue. I must have set the glue lid down on my chair and then forgotten about it—the next thing I knew, I was sitting on it! The lid stuck to my jeans. I pulled and pulled, but couldn't get it off. I didn't know what to do! I definitely couldn't go to my next class with a lid stuck to my pants. So I kept pulling and eventually, the lid came off. Unfortunately, it came off along with a piece of my jeans!

Juanita

LOCKER SURVIVAL KIT

What's the best way to stop embarrassment in its tracks? Always be prepared! And when it comes to school, there's one easy place to gather together all the materials you need to keep your head high when disaster strikes: your locker. Always keep these supplies in your locker—you won't be sorry!

1   **Extra shirt and pair of pants**—To replace anything that stains, rips, falls off, or just looks ridiculous.

2   **Safety pins**—To hold together any piece of clothing that may have come apart. They're the perfect replacement for lost buttons and broken zippers.

3   **Brush**—For those out-of-control hair days.

4   **Hair elastics**—For those *really* out-of-control hair days.

5   **Mirror**—Your best tool in the battle against embarrassment. It's also the best way to check that your teeth, hair, and face are ready to show to the world.

6   **Quarters**—When all else fails and you need to call your mom to come get you!

IT'S NOT EASY BEING GREEN

One night I decided it was time for a change, so I dyed my hair blond. I thought I looked pretty awesome—and in school the next day, everyone agreed. I loved the attention. But that day in gym, we started our swimming unit. When I got out of the pool, my hair was bright green! I tried to wash it out in the shower, but no luck. The rest of the day, I got plenty of attention—but *not* the kind I wanted. To make it worse, the color would not wash out. I had to dye my hair back to brown to cover my green locks!

Meghan

FOR THE BIRDS

I was lying on the beach, about to eat lunch, when a giant flock of seagulls swooped in to attack. They weren't after me—just my lunch. But I still screamed and jumped away from my towel. Everyone on the beach turned to look. I stood there, watching these greedy seagulls devour my lunch. Then someone next to me told me I better check out my hair. I reached up to feel it *and—yuck*! When the seagulls flew over me, they left a little souvenir. I screamed again and raced for the ocean to get it off ASAP!

Dana

CALL THE FASHION POLICE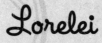

I'm the youngest kid in a big family, and so I always get stuck with hand-me-downs. Sometimes I don't mind. I had one shirt from my oldest sister that I thought was so cool. But the first day I wore it to school, the most popular girl in our class came up to me and said, "Is that your smock for art class?" I wanted to run home right away. As soon as I got home, I threw that shirt under my bed and never wore it again.

Lorelei

YOU'D BETTER SIT DOWN FOR THIS

I was starring in the school play, and it was my big scene. For half the scene I was supposed to be sitting down. For the other half, I was supposed to be dancing. But when I got onstage and sat down, I couldn't believe it—I felt my pants split! I knew I couldn't stand up again. Instead, I made up my lines, saying things like "I'm sorry, I don't like to dance. I'll just talk to you from over here." The other actors didn't know what was going on—until the curtain came down and I finally stood up. Even the audience probably heard their gigantic laughs!

Alexandra

HUMILIATION HELPER:

This is a perfect example of Rule #1 for performing in public: Stay calm and keep going. If you don't freak out and let people know you've messed up, the audience probably won't even notice!

A FULL MOON

Every week in kindergarten, we had story time. We would sit in a circle on a big rug at the front of the class and listen to the teacher tell a story. One day we were all standing around talking, waiting for story time to start. I guess the teacher told us that we were supposed to sit down, but I wasn't paying attention. The boy next to me was already sitting down, and he wanted to keep me from getting in trouble. So he tugged on my shorts to try to get me to sit down. Well, my shorts went down—but I stayed standing!

Barbara

WATCH WHERE YOU SIT

There are a bunch of guys in my school who think it's pretty funny to pull jokes on the rest of us. I usually stay out of their way, but once I wasn't so lucky. I was in the cafeteria, bringing my food back to the table. When I sat down, I heard a weird squishing noise. All the boys at the end of our table started laughing and laughing. I didn't know what to do, so I ignored them. The rest of lunch was normal enough...then I stood up. Everyone behind me roared with laughter— and soon the whole cafeteria had joined in. It turned out that I had sat in a giant puddle of pudding!

Yolanda

HUMILIATION HELPER:

Have you been the victim of a practical joke? It's bad enough when you are laughed at for something that's your fault—it's even worse when it's someone **ELSE'S** fault. That just stinks. But remember—they're probably doing it to be funny, not to be mean. And if you laugh along with them (or at least pretend you're laughing), chances are you won't be their next victim. Practical jokers like victims who will freak out and make a big scene—don't give them what they're looking for!

25

BOY, IS MY FACE...PURPLE

Okay, I admit it. I fell asleep in class—but the class was *really* boring. I woke up when the bell rang and I left with the rest of the class. When I met up with my friends at our lockers, they all gasped. I didn't get it—so they made me look in a mirror. I must have fallen asleep on top of my pen, because there was a giant purple spot on my face! I tried to wash it off, but I only managed to smear it. I had to walk around the rest of the day looking like a grape!

That's what you get for falling asleep in class, young lady!

Bethany

A WORK OF ART

I had some time to kill before meeting my friends at the mall, so I lay down on the couch to watch TV. I must have fallen asleep, because I woke up about an hour later. I was late, so I ran out of the house and headed for the mall. When I saw my friends, they took one look at me and started laughing. They couldn't stop long enough to tell me why, so one of them lent me a mirror. I couldn't believe it! While I was asleep, my little sister had decided to draw—on my face! There was a black beard and mustache drawn on me, along with some red cheeks and purple eyebrows. I tried to get out of the mall without anyone else seeing me—but no such luck.

Ruth

FEELING HOT, HOT, HOT!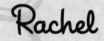

When I got all A's on my report card, my parents took me out to dinner to celebrate. We were about to have dessert when our waiter walked by carrying a pot of coffee. He tripped, and some of it spilled on me. It hurt—but not as much as what happened next! My mother thought the coffee was burning me and she freaked out. So she dumped her glass of ice water on my head. She was also screaming, so the entire restaurant turned toward us to see what was going on. I wasn't burned—just soaking wet and humiliated.

Rachel

UNLUCKY PLUCK

I read in a teen magazine that plucking your eyebrows could make you prettier. So I decided to try it. I asked my mom for help, but she said I was too young—she thought my eyebrows were perfect. What did she know? One day when she was out, I snuck into her room and borrowed her tweezers. Then I raced to the bathroom and started plucking away. It hurt a lot, but I figured no pain, no gain. I plucked, and I plucked, and I plucked—I got a little carried away. By the time I finished, my eyebrows had practically disappeared! When my mother finally found out, she was laughing too hard to be mad. I guess she figured my invisible eyebrows were punishment enough!

Jorie

BUBBLE TROUBLE

My twerpy little brother chews bubble gum. A lot. But the gross part is that when he takes it out, he likes to save it for later, so we're always finding gum around the house—stuck under the kitchen table, on top of the TV, everywhere. One morning when I woke up, my head felt stuck to the pillow— I had a bad feeling I had found another piece of his gum. I was right. My little bro had left gum on my pillow! My hair was all stuck together, and my mother had to cut it out in chunks! It took weeks for my terrible haircut to grow into something normal. It was a *loooong* wait.

Glory

HAIR SURVIVAL KIT

Have you had a hair scare? Find out with this quick and easy hair quiz!

1. **When your hairdresser showed you how your new style looked, did you start to cry?**

2. **Is your new hair color brighter than orange highway cones?**

3. **Are you afraid to go to school in the mornings?**

4. **Does your hair extend more than six inches above your head?**

5. **Do you look like you got your last haircut from your little brother?**

6. ***Did* you get your last haircut from your little brother?**

When you've answered "yes" or "no" to all six questions, turn the page.

If you answered "yes" to even *one* of these questions, then you may have a hair emergency! But worry not—with a hair humiliation survival kit, you have everything you need to save the day (and your reputation). Your kit should include:

Brush, comb, hair dryer, and a fashion-savvy friend—No matter how bad your haircut is, your friend might be able to help.

Hairstylist's number—If you've gotten a terrible haircut, try calling your hairstylist and complaining; she might recut it for free.

Hair bands and bobby pins—For a quick hair-fix when you're on the go, make sure you carry these fixer-uppers.

Ice—Did you (or your annoying younger siblings) get gum in your hair? Try rubbing ice on it—once the gum has frozen, you should be able to chip it off. Some people have also had luck rubbing peanut butter or egg whites on the gum. But ask your parents before raiding the kitchen!

SOUND THE ALARM!

When we have to change after gym, I'm always the slowest one in my class. It's never been much of a problem because I always make it to my next class in time. But once, in the locker room after a swimming class, the fire alarm rang. Everyone else was already dressed, and they ran out—but I was still in my swimsuit. I tried to grab my clothes, but my gym teacher ran through and rushed me out. So I was stuck outside for the next ten minutes—freezing and wearing my swimsuit in front of the whole school!

Nancy

How would YOU rate this humiliation horror story? _____

33

Class Klutz

Like it or not, right now most of your life is spent in school—which means most of your embarrassing moments will probably be there, too. And school is a humiliation hot zone, with plenty of opportunities for tripping up, falling down, and looking just plain ridiculous. But you've got one thing going for you: You can be sure that everyone else has just as much to think about as you do. As embarrassed as you may be by whatever happened, tomorrow everyone will have something new to laugh about. You may never forget that time you fell down in front of your entire gym class—but hopefully the rest of them will!

Humiliation Factor

B BAD, BAD DAY

C CAN'T COME BACK TO SCHOOL FOR A WEEK

D DISASTER. TOTAL DISASTER.

F FACE IT, MY LIFE IS RUINED.

BEHIND THE SCENES D

In our last school play, I had an exciting responsibility: I was in charge of raising and lowering the curtains. To tell you the truth, it was kind of boring—especially after doing it night after night. On the last night of the show, I was so bored that I stopped paying attention—and I missed my cue! I was so flustered that I lowered the curtain as fast as I could. Unfortunately, I lowered the *wrong* curtain. It came down on top of everyone's head—and knocked down the star of the show! The audience loved it; the cast wasn't so happy.

Samantha

SCHOOL'S OUT B

One day my father dropped me off at school. When I went inside, there was no one there. I suddenly remembered that we had the day off because the teachers were going to be in meetings all day. But my dad had already driven away! There was no one to come pick me up, so I had to spend the day sitting in the vice-principal's office, doing my homework and talking to his secretary. The worst part was that the next day, the teachers kept making jokes about how I just couldn't stand to miss a day of school!

Valerie

ROCK 'N' ROLL **D**

I'm the student council president, so after our end-of-the-year party, I stayed behind to clean up the classroom. Since no one was around, I turned on a radio and started singing along. I guess I got a little carried away. When my favorite song came on, I started singing at the top of my lungs and pretending the broom was my guitar. When the song ended, suddenly there was applause. I turned around to see half the student council standing in the doorway. They'd come back to help me clean—but now, all they could do was laugh.

Erica

Rock on!

HEADS UP, HANDS DOWN C

We were playing soccer—*not* my favorite sport—in gym class. I was trying to stay away from the ball, like I always do. For most of the game, it worked. But toward the end, someone kicked the ball right at my face. I put my hands up to block it—and I accidentally caught the ball! In soccer, of course, that's totally *not* allowed. We got a penalty, and the other team got the ball. Right away, they scored the winning goal! The kids on my team wouldn't speak to me for the rest of the class.

Michelle

SILENCE IS GOLDEN B

In my school, everyone is in choir, whether or not they can sing. But for our last choir perform- ance, the music teacher made an exception: me. I have a terrible voice, and I know the teacher hates listening to me sing with the chorus—she must have finally gotten fed up. She said that she thought it would be best if I turned the pages for the piano player instead of singing. She tried to make it seem like I had a special job, but I knew the real reason—and so did the rest of the class!

Maria

ALONG CAME A SPIDER C

We were taking a history test, and the room was totally quiet. Midway through the test, my pencil broke. I knew I had another one in my desk, so I started looking for it. I didn't find my pencil—but I did find a spider! I screamed as loud as I could and jumped out of my chair. Of course, the entire room turned to look at me. The worst part was that it wasn't even a real spider—it was a plastic toy someone had put in my desk as a joke. Some joke!

Frida

CONGRATS, GRAD! F

In sixth grade, I was chosen to give a speech for my elementary school graduation. On the day of graduation, I got up onstage and looked out at the audience. There must have been hundreds of people there—students, teachers, parents—and they were all listening to *me*! I opened my mouth to begin my speech and suddenly realized that my nose was bleeding all over my white dress and on the note cards with my speech written on them! I tried to keep going, but the vice-principal came up and made me sit down. Things got even worse: Someone's dad was taping the graduation, and he sent the tape into one of those TV series that shows embarrassing videos. It was the worst moment of my life—and the entire country saw it!

Luma

GET OUT OF SCHOOL
Free PASS

Okay, so you made an unbelievable, gigantic, horrible, humiliating fool of yourself at school today. And now you're shut in your room and you're not coming out until college. Or maybe law school. There's only one problem with that plan—Mom and Dad probably won't be thrilled. And sadly, telling them that you're dying of humiliation most likely won't convince them to give you the rest of the decade off. What *will* work? Try these excuses*:

"How about I stay home from school and clean the entire house, top to bottom, and do everyone's laundry for a week?"

"My teacher got the bubonic plague, so he said we should all stay home today."

"I'll pay you half my allowance if
you let me stay home."

"Cough. Cough.
I think I have pneumonia. Cough."

"I hear there's a tornado coming—maybe,
just to be safe, we should stay inside."

"Didn't you hear on the news last night? The
school's been sold—they're turning it
into a mall."

*This is, of course, a joke. You must go to school. Every day.
School is good for you. Even when you think it's going to stink.
Okay, even when it does stink. Which it sometimes does.
But you'll never make it to college—or law school— unless
you make it through K–12!

LOST AND FOUND 13

For months, I had been begging my parents to let me walk home from school, just like the other kids. They didn't think I was old enough, but I knew I could do it. One day, they finally agreed. I was so excited. After school, I set off toward home. Or, at least, I *thought* I was walking toward home. I was wrong. An hour later, I was still walking. I walked around for two hours before I gave up—by then I was hot, sweaty, and in tears. I went into the nearest store and called my mom for a ride home. When she found me, she laughed—I was only three blocks from my house!

Gajra

HUMILIATION HELPER:

Here's a rule to live by: Whenever you're going somewhere new on your own, make sure you know where you're going. This may sound like a no-brainer, but there's a difference between **KNOWING** where you're going and **THINKING** you know where you're going. So look at a map (or, better yet, bring one with you!) and plan your route ahead of time.

And when all else fails, there's an easy way out: Stop and ask for directions!

44

ON THE AIR F

My school has a TV station. Every morning, we broadcast the news to all the homerooms. I'm one of the reporters, which I usually love. But one day, I was feeling really sick—as soon as I got to school, I knew I should have stayed home. But since I was there, I had to do the news that morning. I made it through the broadcast—barely. As soon as we were done, I totally lost it. I puked all over the news desk! I was so embarrassed and grossed out—but I figured that at least I had held it in until the broadcast was over. That's when I realized that the little green light on the camera was still on. We were on the air—and the whole school had seen me throw up. I was out sick for the rest of the week, but I didn't mind—no way did I want to go back to school!

Faith

PSST... C

My best friend and I were bored in class (like always), so we were writing notes back and forth. Toward the end of class, I wrote a note to her and kicked it across the floor. Unfortunately my teacher, Mrs. Spinella, caught me—and the note. She made me get up in front of the class and read the note out loud. I bet she wished she hadn't. The note read: "Dear Katie, this class is BORING. And can you believe that Mrs. Spinella's zipper has been down this whole time?" I was so embarrassed—but not half as embarrassed as Mrs. Spinella!

Zoe

YOU'VE GOT THE PART! C

I was really nervous about auditioning for the school musical—I had never sung in public before. But I really wanted a part. At the audition, we were allowed to sing any song we wanted, and I had memorized all the words to my favorite song. But when I got up onstage and saw all those people, I totally blanked out. I couldn't remember my song—or any song. The only thing I could remember were the words to a laundry detergent jingle. So that's what I sang! I was so humiliated, I thought I'd never have the nerve to get on a stage again—but then I got the part!

Marissa

HUMILIATION HELPER:

So you have an audition for something you really, really want. And, of course, you're scared out of your mind.

First things first: Try to stop worrying that you're going to mess up. If you do, it won't be the worst thing in the world—and if you worry too much about it, you might make it happen.

Next: You know all those butterflies in your stomach? Why not make them work for you? Use all the nervous energy you have to look excited and energetic onstage. Smile, look out at the audience, talk clearly, or sing loudly. You can't control how much talent you have, but you can control how much enthusiasm you have. And if you have a lot—if the director sees that you've got real "stage presence"—you'll have a good chance of getting a part!

Do, re, mi...

BONJOUR, MONSIEUR 13

When a foreign exchange student came to our class, the teacher picked me to show her around. I figured that this was a great chance to practice my French, so I tried to say a bunch of things to her in French. She didn't say anything back to me—and she started looking really confused. I began to wonder if there was something wrong with her. Finally, she interrupted me and in perfect English said, "I'm sorry, I don't speak French—I am from Spain." I guess I wasn't paying attention when the teacher told us where she was from!

Asahiko

EMBARRASSMENT Around the World

Next time you say the wrong thing around your foreign exchange student, you'll be able to say "I'm embarrassed" in the language of your choice!

French—Je suis embarrassée

Spanish—Me da vergüenza

German—Ich geniere mich

Portuguese—Tenho vergonho

Russian—Mne stidna

49

LAST STOP D

I needed to do some research for a school term paper, and the book that I needed wasn't in our school library. So I convinced my parents to let me go to the public library by myself after school. It should have been easy—there's a city bus that stops right in front of the library. This was the first time I'd ever taken a bus by myself (except for the school bus), so I felt very proud. I got on the bus, and waited for my stop to come. I waited...and waited...and waited. Then the bus driver announced the last stop, and everyone got off the bus but me. When I asked him about the library, it turned out that I was on the wrong bus—and I was stranded across town! I didn't have enough money to pay for the ride back, and I didn't know what to do—so I just started to cry. The bus driver felt bad for me and gave me a free ride back. When I got off, I was so embarrassed I forgot to thank him!

Dara

AND THE WINNER IS... **F**

At the end of the year, my school has an awards ceremony at which awards are given to the best students. One person wins the Outstanding Student Prize, which comes with $100. I really wanted it—and I couldn't wait for the winner to be announced. Finally, at the end of the ceremony, they announced it. All I heard was "Chavonne"—my name—and I jumped up and started walking toward the stage. But then another girl named Chavonne got up, too. I realized that they hadn't called my name—they'd called hers. Not only did I lose out on the award, but I embarrassed myself in front of the entire school!

Chavonne

XTREME HUMILIATION

WET AND WILD

I was washing my hands in the girls' bathroom when the faucet suddenly went out of control. Water was spraying everywhere! By the time I backed away, it was too late—my pants were soaking wet. I couldn't go back to class, so I went to the nurse's office. I had to sit there and wait for my mother to bring new pants and underwear. And when people found out I was in the nurse's office waiting for a new pair of pants, you know what they thought. I tried to tell them that I hadn't had an "accident"—but, of course, no one believed me!

Erin

How would YOU rate this
humiliation horror story? _____

With Friends Like These

What are friends for? They're always around—to talk to, to joke with, to laugh with, to laugh at you... Wait a second, they're not supposed to laugh *at* you!

But of course they *do*. And you know it's true (because you've laughed at them once or twice, too). Every once in a while, you do something silly around your friends—and they just can't help themselves. Try not to get upset—after all, it'll be their turn soon enough!

Humiliation Factor

 AT LEAST THIS FRIENDSHIP IS NEVER BORING!

I'LL ALWAYS BE YOUR FRIEND—JUST DON'T TELL ANYONE I KNOW YOU!

I KNOW WE'RE BFF—BUT IS FOREVER OVER YET?

 FRIENDS THROUGH THICK AND THIN—BUT NOT THROUGH THIS!

53

TRICK OR TREAT!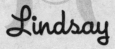

This year, my friends and I decided we were too old to go trick-or-treating for Halloween. I didn't know what I would do instead, so I was really excited to get an invitation to my first-ever Halloween party. I decided to dress as a witch. I got a long black wig, fake nails, and some bright green face paint. I thought I looked pretty good—until I got to the party. I was the only one there in a costume! Apparently everyone else had decided we were also too old to dress up—too bad no one mentioned it to me.

Lindsay

HUMILIATION HELPER:

Here's a tip that should help you steer clear of some potentially painful moments: Get by with a little help from your friends.

Your friends may be fun to have around, but that's not their only purpose. They're also there to keep you from embarrassing yourself. Let's face it: No one can make good decisions 100% of the time. Even you.

So when you're about to make a big decision—whether it's dyeing your hair purple, buying a bright orange vest, or painting your face in the school colors to support the chess team in their big tournament—ask your friends what they think.

Do you have to listen to them? No way. Once in a while, though, your friends may have something useful to tell you—like which brands of hair dye will make your hair fall out, or the fact that you have a big piece of spinach stuck in your teeth. Hey, it never hurts to ask!

THREE STRIKES AND YOU'RE OUT

Sometimes my friends and I play softball. Even though I'm not a great player, it's always a lot of fun. Once I was up at bat, with one out left. I hit the ball as hard as I could and it went sailing away—a home run! I ran around the bases as fast as I could, and no one tried to stop me. But when I crossed home plate, no one cheered. They just stared at me. It turns out that it wasn't a home run after all. It was a foul ball—but I'd hit it so hard that it had flown into the trees next to our field. That was the end of our game that day!

Malika

Take her out to the ball game more often!

L.O.L.

My friends and I talk on the Internet all the time—IM'ing is much better than talking on the phone. Or so I thought. One day, I saw that my friend Jim was online and I IM'ed him to say hello. I got an IM back saying "This isn't Jim, this is Jim's mother." Jim is a big joker, so I figured this was just another joke. I decided I could be funny, too. I wrote back that it couldn't be his mother because he'd said she wasn't smart enough to use a computer. It was just a joke, but it turned out the joke was on me, because it *was* his mother. Oops.

Fatima

HUMILIATION HELPER:
Want to steer clear of online embarrassment? Here's a tip: Never say anything online that you wouldn't say out loud. E-mail and IM may **SEEM** private—but just remember, you never really know who's on the other end!

DINNER ONLY A DOG COULD LOVE

I'm a *very* picky eater, so when my friend invited me to her house for dinner, I was a little worried that I wouldn't like what they served. I was right to be worried. Dinner was some sort of meat that I had never seen before. I had never tasted anything like it—and I never wanted to taste anything like it again! So I used a trick my little brother taught me: Whenever I could, I snuck pieces of my dinner into my napkin and then slipped them into my pocket. Obviously, I could not clear my plate that way—but I could get rid of enough so that her parents wouldn't think I was rude. Unfortunately, my friend has a dog— and as soon as we got up from the dinner table, the dog jumped on me. No one could understand why, but I knew—it wanted the meat in my pocket. It's a giant dog, and it took both my friend's parents to pull it off of me. When they did, they saw what the dog had pulled out of my pocket—a napkin stuffed with meat!

Elaine

PLAYING DRESS UP

I'm kind of a tomboy, and my mother is always very excited when she gets the chance to stick me in a dress. When I got invited to my friend Alison's elementary school graduation party, my mom figured she had her chance. I tried to tell her that kids don't get dressed up for parties anymore, but she didn't believe me. I rang Alison's doorbell wearing a brand-new party dress. Alison answered the door wearing jeans and a T-shirt—just like every other kid there. It turns out that Alison has a pool, and this was a swim party! No one could believe that I, of all people, was wearing a dress. I couldn't believe it, either. I had to borrow one of Alison's old bathing suits for the rest of the party. It was incredibly ugly—but anything was better than that dress!

Colleen

PARTY SURVIVAL KIT

Parties can be rough—you never know quite what you're in for until you get there, which means there's always a chance you'll be wearing the wrong thing. And then once you're there, who knows what could happen? Someone could spill punch on you, you could fall on top of someone else—it's a party, *anything* could happen! So should you stay home and watch TV for the rest of your life? No way—but you should definitely make sure you're ready with these necessary accessories for whatever a party can throw at you:

1 **Piece of jewelry**—Underdressed? The right necklace, bracelet, or earrings can fix your too-casual look and make you totally glam.

2 **Hair band**—Overdressed? Add a funky ponytail or a fun barrette to dress down your outfit.

3 **Smile**—Whatever you're wearing, look like you mean it—you're not dressed wrong, everyone else at the party is. Who knows, maybe you'll start a new style!

SWEET DREAMS

I couldn't believe it when the most popular girl in school invited me to a sleepover at her house. And the house was beautiful, especially her bedroom—it was all pink and white and ruffled. She let me sleep on her bed, and she slept on a cot next to me. I loved her bed, especially the pillow, which was pink and lacy. We talked until 3 AM and then went to sleep. When I woke up, she was standing over me, looking disgusted. "You ruined it!" she said, pointing down at the pillow. I turned to see what she was looking at—I had drooled in my sleep, and there was a giant stain of saliva on her fancy pillow! The next day in school she told everyone that I drooled like a baby. I guess I just wasn't meant to be popular.

Nina

AH-CHOO!

I was having lunch with my best friend. When the food came, she got up to wash her hands and I was left at the table by myself. Suddenly, I had a sneezing attack and—I can barely admit it—I sneezed all over the table, including her food. I didn't know what to do! I was too embarrassed to tell her about it. When she came back, I didn't say anything. I just sat there and let her eat—and the whole time, she kept saying how good the food was!

Laurie

Gesundheit!

JUST CLOWNING AROUND

For my last birthday, I wanted to have a roller-skating party, but the rink was closed that day. I was really disappointed, but my mother said she'd make it up to me. She promised me a birthday party I'd never forget. On the day of the party, everything was going well—we were all having a great time, and I had almost forgotten my mother's surprise. Then the doorbell rang. I opened the door—and a clown burst into the room. That's right, my mother had actually hired a *clown* for my birthday party! I wished a giant hole would open up in the floor and suck me into it. But no such luck. Instead, I had to stand there in front of all my friends while the lame clown sang "Happy Birthday." Maybe next year, I'll skip the party.

Beth

How would YOU rate this humiliation horror story? _____

Boy Trouble

Boys! They're never around when you need them—and just when you wish they'd disappear, there they are. There's nothing worse than embarrassing yourself in front of the one person you want to impress the most. But don't worry. There's one thing you can count on about boys: They don't notice much. And if you do have a horrible moment that they just can't miss—whether you spill on them, spit on them, or drool on them—at least you'll make them notice *you*!

Humiliation Factor

 BOY BLUNDER

UNLUCKY IN LOVE

A *CRUSH*-ING BLOW

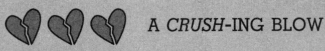 **HEARTBREAKING HUMILIATION**

LOOK WHO'S TALKING

I really, really, really liked this boy in my class, so I decided to ask him to the movies. It took me a long time to work up the nerve. But one day, I finally called and asked him. I couldn't believe it—he actually said yes! We arranged to meet in the theater lobby the next day at four. But when I met him there, he looked totally surprised to see me. Then he said, "Oh, that was you on the phone—I thought it was the other Julie. Too bad." The other Julie in our class is the most popular girl in school—and he was clearly wishing I was her! We sat through the movie together, but I was too embarrassed to talk to him for the rest of the year.

*What makes you think I'd ever go out with **you**?*

Julie

LET'S PRETEND

I have two little sisters, and they love to play make-believe in the backyard. I play with them sometimes, because it makes them so happy. One day we were pretending—they were space explorers and I was the spaceship. I was zooming through the yard with my arms stretched out, shouting things like "Zoom, zoom, whoosh!" when I heard someone laugh. And it didn't sound like my little sisters. I looked up to see our new neighbor watching us. He was supercute and looked like he was about my age—but he must have thought *I* looked like a five-year-old.

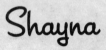

Shayna

MAN OVERBOARD!

When my family went on vacation in Florida this year, my parents let me take a sailing lesson. I was psyched to learn how to sail—and even more psyched to meet my sailing instructor, a total hottie. I couldn't wait to spend an hour on the boat, just him and me. But there was one problem with my plan: I was a terrible sailor. I couldn't understand anything he was telling me—and I was also getting seasick. At one point, a really big wave swept me over the side of the boat, and I ended up in the water. My instructor reached over to help me—but I accidentally pulled him in, too! When we got back to shore, we were both soaking wet.

Jamie

AMERICAN IDOL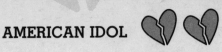

I'd heard that in New York, you always see celebrities on the street—so I wasn't surprised when I went to New York and saw one. My friend and I were walking down the street when we passed Tom Cruise! He was even hotter in person than he is in the movies. I couldn't believe it was him—and before I knew what I was doing, I stopped him and asked for his autograph. He looked at me strangely, but he gave me his autograph. Once he walked away, my friend burst out laughing and clued me in. It turns out that it *wasn't* Tom Cruise—or anyone famous at all. I didn't believe her until I looked at the autograph. He'd signed "Mike Cohen—thanks for making me feel famous!"

Joanna

DROOL FOOL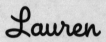

Most people hate going to the dentist, but I love it. Why? Because a very cute boy in school goes to the same dentist I do, and sometimes we're there on the same afternoon. Last time I went, I had to get some cavities filled. The pain was totally worth it. When I finished, I saw the cute guy in the waiting room. I sat down to talk to him, and he was so great. He even got us both a drink of water, like a real gentleman. Unfortunately, I still had a lot of Novocain in my mouth. When I took a sip of my water, half of it dribbled back out again—right onto his lap! He laughed about it, but I could tell he was totally grossed out.

Lauren

WATCH YOUR STEP

At our Spring Fling this year, I was asked to slow dance for the first time. I was so excited—too bad I don't really know how to dance. I stepped on the boy's toes on almost every beat. By the end of the dance, I think he may have been limping! After the dance, he told all the other boys to stay away from me—and for the rest of the month, everyone in school called me "Bigfoot"!

Hayley

HAIR SCARE

I never turn down a dare—or at least I never used to. At the last sleepover party I went to, we played Truth or Dare. I picked Dare, of course. My friend dared me to take a slow walk around the block—dressed in my pajamas and her mother's hair curlers. I figured no big deal, so I did it. It would have been no big deal, except that halfway around the block, a car pulled up next to me. My brother's best friend—the captain of the high school football team—leaned out to say hello. I've had a crush on him *forever*! He took one look at me and my outfit and started laughing hysterically. I put my hands over my face and ran back to my friend's house as fast as I could. That's my last game of Truth or Dare for a long time!

Zhen

IM = INSTANT M-BARRASSMENT

My friends and I send IM's to one another all the time, so when I found out the online name of my crush, I kept saying I was going to IM him. But, of course, I was too wimpy to actually do it. One day my best friend was at my house, playing on my computer. When I wasn't looking, she went online and started chatting with my crush—using *my* name! She told him how much I liked him and even asked him out! I was going to kill her, until she pointed at the screen. He'd said yes!

Karen

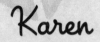

HUMILIATION HELPER:

Got a crush on an incredibly cute guy? What's your game plan? You could do your best to make sure that he never, ever finds out that you're interested: Swear your friends to secrecy, tape your little sister's mouth shut, save your confessions of love for your diary, and try to say as little as possible in Mr. Right's presence.

Okay—but where's it going to get you? If you keep this up, the guy of your dreams might never know you exist. Or, if he does, he'll probably think you hate him (why else would you and your friends be whispering and giggling to one another every time he walks by)?

If you don't have the nerve to just walk up to the object of your affection and ask him out, don't worry. You don't have to tell him you like him—just help him guess. Start conversations with him when you get the chance; tell him you like the shirt he's wearing, or you think his new haircut is cool; ask him about things that interest him and tell him about things that interest you. In other words, take some time to get to know him, and help him get to know you.

Perhaps he has a big crush on you, too, but he's too scared to do anything about it. Maybe, maybe not—there's only one way to find out. This is the perfect solution—there's no risk of embarrassing yourself, and whatever else happens, you'll probably end up with a new friend!

P-U! IS THAT YOU?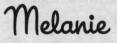

I was waiting for an elevator in the lobby of my doctor's office. Finally, it came. The man on it brushed past me on his way out—he smelled worse than anything I've smelled in my entire life! I got on the elevator and, just as the doors were closing, I noticed that the elevator smelled just like he did. It was too late to get out, so I tried holding my breath. The elevator stopped on the next floor, and this incredibly cute guy got on. I smiled at him, but he just made a weird face at me and looked away. That's when I realized—there was no one else on the elevator, so he must have thought the smell was coming from me! That was the longest elevator ride of my life!

Melanie

LOVE LETTERS

One day, our teacher gave us a pop quiz. I finished early, and pretty soon I was bored, so I started daydreaming. Of course, I started day-dreaming about Alex, my crush. He's so cute. Suddenly, I realized that I had been doodling Alex's name with little hearts around it all over my test paper. I was so embarrassed—but I thought that maybe my teacher wouldn't notice. At least she would be the only one to see it. Then my teacher announced that we should exchange papers with the person sitting next to us to check each other's work. Well, guess who sits next to me—Alex! I couldn't believe it—I actually had to hand my quiz to him!

Nicole

How would YOU rate this humiliation horror story? _____

All in the Family

Why does your family seem determined to embarrass you? You know they love you—so why does their every move seem calculated to make you the laughingstock of the world? There's only one thing that can give you comfort. Everyone has parents—so everyone knows what you're dealing with. Just take a look at these families (and be glad you're not a part of them!).

Humiliation Factor

 FAMILIES. CAN'T LIVE WITH THEM, CAN'T AFFORD YOUR OWN HOUSE.

 WOULD IT BE OUT OF THE QUESTION TO PITCH A TENT IN THE BACKYARD?

I DON'T KNOW THESE PEOPLE, I SWEAR.

 IS IT TOO SOON TO LEAVE FOR COLLEGE?

WHAT'S UP, DOC?

Once I went to the movies with my friends and my mother said she'd pick us up after her office party. Unfortunately, she hadn't mentioned that this party was a *costume* party—and she wasn't planning on changing before she came to get us. So when I saw her in the lobby of the movie theater, I didn't recognize her at first—she was dressed as a giant bunny! I couldn't figure out why there would be a giant bunny in the lobby...until it started waving and calling my name. I'll never live that one down!

Abbie

If You Can't Beat 'Em, JOIN 'EM!

Whoever said "laughter is the best medicine" knew what he was talking about.

So everyone's laughing at you?

So what?

Why not laugh right along with them (even if laughing is the last thing in the world you feel like doing)? If you have a sense of humor about yourself, you may find that people are laughing with you, rather than at you.

That doesn't mean you have to turn yourself into a clown. But don't take yourself too seriously, either. If you've done something totally silly, be the first to admit it and laugh along with everyone else. Who knows—you might actually decide it *was* funny!

DESPERATELY SEEKING SARAH

Usually when I'm out, my mother will call me on my cell phone if she needs to change the time she's picking me up. But when I go to the movies, I turn off my cell—big mistake. The last time I was at the movies, the movie suddenly stopped in the middle. We were all wondering what had happened, when the PA system came on. "Sarah Hudson, please call your mother. Sarah Hudson, call your mother right now." Everyone looked around to see who Sarah Hudson was. Unfortunately, they were about to find out—I ran out of the theater and called home, begging my mother to never, ever do that again!

Sarah

HOUSE OF STYLE

My parents both work, so after school I sometimes have to baby-sit my little brother. Usually I bring a friend home and we watch TV while my little brother does whatever it is that little brothers do. Well, *this* time, my friend was the cutest boy in our class, and I was so excited. We were doing our homework in the living room when it happened. My brother came running down the stairs—dressed in my best dress, my shoes, and wearing a pair of *my* underwear on his head! I was dying of embarrassment, and my cute new friend just laughed and laughed and laughed.

Mei

Does anyone out there want a little brother?

BABY TALK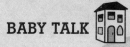

Whenever I had the day off from school, my mother used to take me to her office. I hate it there—it's totally boring, and I have to make small talk with her coworkers. The last time I went there, my mother made me promise to be nice to her friends and try to make conversation. Well, I was trying to talk to one of them, and I asked her when her baby was due. Turns out she wasn't pregnant! I wasn't nearly as embarrassed as my mother was. Like I said, that's the *last* time I went there!

Claire

HUMILIATION HELPER:

You just had to do it, didn't you? You opened your big mouth—and look what came out! When your mouth gets you in trouble, you may be tempted to use it to help you get **OUT** of trouble, but that's not always the best thing to try. If you stammer around trying to make things better, you may only make them worse.

Instead, try to look embarrassed (you'll probably take care of that without trying) and just apologize. If you said something **REALLY** stupid, then apologize a lot. It may not work—but at least you tried!

I LOVE YOU, YOU LOVE ME

One day I was late for school, and I accidentally grabbed my little sister's backpack instead
of my own. I didn't notice until it was too late. I
had to go through the whole day using her pink
unicorn binder and her fluffy purple pencil. And,
of course, my friends will never let me forget the
stuffed Barney doll that popped out of the bag
when I opened it in the middle of math class.

Sadguna

JOLLY GREEN GIANT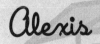

Last summer, my family went on vacation to a cabin in the mountains. We went swimming as soon as we got there, and it was the first time I ever swam in a lake. I wasn't impressed. The lake was muddy and there were actually *fish* in it! Suddenly, I felt something cold and slimy brush against my leg—and then it trapped me and started pulling me down. I started to scream—I was convinced that a giant green sea monster had me! Everyone in the lake came swimming over to help. When they reached me, they discovered that I *had* been trapped by something giant and green—algae. The next day, when my family went for a swim, I stayed in the cabin and watched TV.

Alexis

A STAR IS BORN

My school play was *Snow White*, and I was the star. My whole family came to see me, including my four-year-old brother. The show turned out to be a little too much for him. When I took a bite out of the poisoned apple, I pretended to faint. But my brother thought it was for real and he freaked out. Before my parents could stop him, he ran up onstage and knocked over half the sets on his way to me. That was one play that didn't end happily ever after.

Jina

HUMILIATION HELPER:

So your little brother or little sister is determined to ruin your life? Join the club. How are you supposed to keep them from totally humiliating you in front of family, friends, and—in the worst-case scenario—the entire world? You've got some options:

THREATS: Sure you can threaten a bratty sib with punishment, but you run a big risk: They can always run and tell Mom and Dad. Guess who gets punished then?

REVENGE: This may sound good, but it has a painful tendency to backfire. And you could be the one to get grounded—and little bro or sis will have the last laugh after all.

BRIBERY: Possibly the perfect solution. You know little kids want a lot of stuff—chances are, there's something they want to do more than embarrassing you. Is a friend coming over to your house after school? Tell your little sis that if she behaves herself, you'll finally agree to have that doll's tea party she's been whining about. Or tell your little bro he can use your stereo to listen to music. No yelling, no screaming, no humiliation—and as a bonus, you'll score extra points from your parents!

85

VACATION SURVIVAL KIT

When you go on vacation, you may leave your troubles behind—but you bring your family with you. Having your family around 24/7 can be fun—but it can also be incredibly annoying. And, sometimes, incredibly embarrassing. Don't worry—as long as you pack well, you'll have everything you need to protect yourself from disasters-on-the-go! Here's a list of some travel essentials.

1   **Snacks**—Wherever you go, you'll probably be hungry when you get there (and who knows what the food situation will be?).

2   **Suntan lotion**—A must, if you're going somewhere sunny. You don't want to look like a lobster when you get back home.

3   **Skirt**—You never know what's going to happen on a vacation. If someone decides to sweep you off to the ball, you want to be prepared!

4 **Books, magazines**—Total boredom busters.

5 **Headphones**—Perfect for blocking out whiny little brothers when you need a break.

LOOK, BUT DON'T TOUCH

My parents love to go shopping for antiques, and sometimes they take me with them. One time, we were in a tiny store that sold little glass animals, and I was bored out of my mind. I turned around to tell my parents that I would wait for them outside—but I must have brushed against one of the glass animals, because suddenly I heard a crash. I looked down, and there was glass all around me. The shop owner came running over and started yelling, "You break it, you buy it!" By this point, everyone in the store was looking at us. I figured that my parents would just pay for it and yell at me later, but no such luck. Instead, my father started yelling *back* at the shop owner, claiming that "you break it, you buy it" is illegal. (Of course, he had no idea whether that was true or not.) The shop owner threw us out of the store! And my mother usually yells at *me* for making a scene. What were they thinking?

Nora

HAPPY BIRTHDAY!

   On my birthday last year, my mother sent me
to school promising that there'd be a special surprise waiting for me afterward. I could barely sit
through the day, wondering what my surprise
would be. The final bell rang, and I ran out to
the parking lot to wait for my mother to come
pick me up. I didn't have to wait long. My mother
pulled up in our minivan—it was covered in
streamers and balloons and a big sign that read
HAPPY BIRTHDAY, HILARY! All the kids started laughing, and, meanwhile, my mother was honking
and waving at me. She looked like she had given
me the best birthday present in the world. For her
sake, I tried to smile. I didn't want her to see that
inside, I was dying of embarrassment.

REVENGE GONE WRONG

My little brother is always hiding my stuff. He doesn't listen when I tell him to stop, so I decided to get some revenge. He has an ugly blue "blankie" that he carries around everywhere. So one day while he was napping, I snuck into his room and took the blankie—I hid it in my back-pack, thinking that was the last place he would look. I was right! I "helped" him look for it all night long but—surprise, surprise—we couldn't find it anywhere. Unfortunately, I forgot about the whole thing when I left for school the next morn-ing. At least, I forgot until I pulled my notebook out of the bag—and the blankie came out with it. The rest of the class thought it was the funniest thing they'd ever seen—I'm just glad my brother wasn't there to see it!

Natalie

FAMILY MATTERS

Every summer, we stay with my grandmother at her beach house, which is great. I love getting to spend the time with my grandmother—usually. But she does strange things sometimes. At night, she wraps her head in toilet paper and bobby pins to keep her hair straight. This is okay, as long as no one else sees her. But one day I went out with my friends and came home a little later than I was supposed to. When my friends dropped me off at my house, my grandmother was pacing back and forth on the porch—wearing toilet paper on her head. In front of everyone, she started yelling at me for staying out so late. I just wanted to bury my head in the sand!

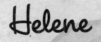

Helene

WILL YOU BE MY FRIEND?

My aunt Millie lives by the ocean, so when we visit her, we sometimes go to the beach. I usually just hang out with my family all day because I don't know anyone there. This is fine with me, but it's not fine with my aunt—she always thinks I should be hanging out with kids my own age. Her solution? She goes up to strange kids and says, "That's my niece over there, and she doesn't have any friends—will you go play with her?" Then she drags them over to talk to me—it's sooooo embarrassing!

Sherry

UNDERWEAR SCARE

The department store near us was having a big sale, so my mother dragged me there to buy all the things she thought I needed. While I was waiting for her to finish shopping, I ran into Mr. Brown, our cute substitute science teacher. He stopped to say hello to me, and we talked about school. Just as I was thinking how jealous all my friends would be, my mother came back—carrying an armful of underwear for me. Even more embarrassing was that I just wanted to get out of there, but then my mother insisted on staying to talk to Mr. Brown. It seemed like we were there forever!

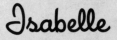

Isabelle

ARE YOU WITH ME?

I was shopping with my mother when I saw that my absolute favorite store was having a sale. I rushed over, with my mother following close behind me. Finally, I saw it: the best shirt in the store. The shirt I *had* to have. Just one problem: It was way more money than my mother would want to spend. So I started begging her for it. "Please, please, please," I said, "I love this shirt. I'll do anything for it!" I turned around to see how it was working—and it was working fine, except my mother wasn't behind me anymore. It was a salesperson! She laughed and said I was welcome to have any shirt I wanted . . . as long as I paid her for it. I haven't been back to that store for a long time.

XTREME HUMILIATION

LET'S BOOGIE

When I went to my first boy–girl dance, my parents came along to help chaperone. I begged them not to—but they wouldn't listen. I finally just made them promise to stay out of the way. I should have known that would never work. For the first half of the dance, no one was dancing—except my parents. They were going wild on the dance floor, and *everyone* was watching them! Later that night, a big group of kids was standing around laughing and pointing at something in the corner. I was afraid to look—and I should have been. There were my parents in the corner—kissing. Gross!

Chante

Do parents ever grow up?

How would YOU rate this humiliation horror story? _____

The End of the Road

Well, that's it. You've read all the stories and all the advice—and hopefully, you've come across some stories even more miserable than your own. Has it helped you suffer through your embarrassment?

If not, there's just one thing left to do: Wait it out.

Embarrassment only lasts so long. One day, no matter what, you'll wake up to find that you've put it behind you, whatever it was. You've moved on. And you will vow that you will never, ever, ever do something so embarrassing again.

Great plan. One problem: It'll never work. And when it fails—as it totally will—don't forget what you know now. Embarrassment doesn't last forever—whatever happens, you'll get through it!